Whales and Dolphins

Susanna Davidson

Designed by Nelupa Hussain
and Catherine-Anne MacKinnon

Illustrated by John Woodcock
Consultant: Sónia Mendes

NN

MANCHESTER
CITY COUNCIL

Please return/renew this item
by the last date shown.
Books may also be renewed by
phone or the Internet.

Tel: 0161 254 7777
www.manchester.gov.uk/libraries

Contents

4 Underwater mammals

6 Whale bodies

8 Swimming

10 Basic senses

12 Underwater sounds

14 Dolphin brains

16 Breathing

18 Feeding

20 Finding a mate

22 Whale babies

24 Living in groups

26 Whale travel

28 Whales and people

30 Enormous whales

32 Right and gray whales

34 Deep-water whales

36 Arctic whales

38 Oceanic dolphins

40 Killers and pilots

42 River dolphins

44 Amazing facts

46 Index

47 Usborne Quicklinks

Usborne Quicklinks

The Usborne Quicklinks Website is packed with links to all the best websites on the Internet. To visit the recommended websites for this book, go to

www.usborne-quicklinks.com
and enter the keywords:
discovery whales

Pictures in this book marked with a ★ can also be downloaded from Quicklinks for school or personal use.

When using the internet please follow the internet safety guidelines displayed on the Usborne Quicklinks Website.

Cover picture: a killer whale leaping out of the water
Title page: humpback whale tail
This page: bottlenose dolphins

Underwater mammals

Whales are among the largest and most intelligent animals living in the sea. Many people think of dolphins as being different from whales, but they are actually a kind of small whale. Whales live in seas and oceans all over the world, and some dolphins live in rivers.

These are bottlenose dolphins. They are very playful and often leap and somersault out of the water like this.

Family matters

There are two main types of whales: whales with teeth, called toothed whales, and whales without teeth, called baleen whales. Scientists also divide up different kinds, or species, of whales into families. Species that share similar features belong to the same family.

Mammals

Whales look similar to sharks and other fish, but are actually more closely related to people. Whales belong to a group of animals called mammals. Mammals can't breathe underwater, so whales have to come to the surface to breathe.

This diagram shows the main baleen and toothed whale families.

Toothed whales

Sperm whale families

Beaked whale family

Dolphin family

Baleen whales

Rorqual whale family

Gray whale family

Narwhal and beluga family

Right whale family

Porpoise family

Pygmy right whale family

River dolphin families

★

Little and large

The largest whales are blue whales. They can grow longer than three buses and weigh about the same as 25 elephants. However, not all whales are enormous. The porpoise family has some of the smallest whales, many of them smaller than people.

Sleek shapes

All whales have sleek, streamlined bodies, which means that their shape allows them to move easily through the water. But whales can still look very different from each other. Sperm whales, for example, have dark, wrinkled skin, while belugas are smooth and white.

Intelligent creatures

Many people are interested in dolphins because they appear to be very intelligent. Dolphins have large brains for the size of their bodies and are good at solving problems. Some people even believe that dolphins have their own language.

This is a sperm whale. They have the largest heads of any animal.

Whale bodies

There are around eighty different species of whales. Although whales come in many different shapes and sizes, they all share a few important features which help them to live and move around underwater.

The ear openings are behind the eyes.

Snout

This is a humpback whale. Humpback whales can be found in oceans all over the world. The labels show the features common to most whales.

Blubbery bodies

Heat escapes from bodies much more quickly in water than in air. So whales have a thick layer of fat, known as blubber, under their skin to keep them warm. Whales that live in cold water have a thicker layer of blubber.

Teeth and bristles

Some species of toothed whales only have a few teeth in their mouths, while others have as many as 260. Instead of teeth, baleen whales have large bristles, which hang down from their upper jaws. The bristles grow together in clumps, called baleen plates.

You can see this bottlenose dolphin's teeth, as it opens its snout to bite some food.

This is a close-up of a gray whale's baleen plates. They have up to 360 in their mouths.

This is a dorsal fin. Most whales have one on their backs.

Whale tails

The most obvious difference between whales and fish is their tails. All fish have vertical tails which they move from side to side as they swim, whereas whales have horizontal tails which they move up and down.

Whale tail

Shark tail

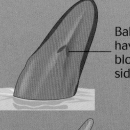

A shark is a type of fish. Here you can see the difference between a shark's and a whale's tail.

This is a flipper. Whales have two flippers, one on each side, which they use for turning, steering and balance.

Internet links

For links to exciting websites about this subject, go to **www.usborne-quicklinks.com** and enter the keywords "discovery whales".

The end of the tail is made up of two sections called flukes.

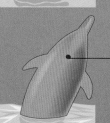

Baleen whales have two blowholes side by side.

Breathing through blowholes

Whales can't breathe through their mouths as we do. Instead, they breathe through small holes, called blowholes, on the tops of their heads. This means they can breathe without raising their heads far above the surface. Baleen whales have two blowholes and toothed whales have one.

Toothed whales have one blowhole, usually in the middle of the head.

 Fact: Humpback whales have longer flippers than any other whale. They can be up to 5m (16.5ft) long.

Swimming

Whales are amazing swimmers. Their tails, flippers, smooth skin and body shape all help them to move easily and quickly through water. They need to be able to swim well to search for food and to escape from animals that might try to attack them.

These are spotted dolphins. They are fast swimmers and often swim close together like this for safety.

Power strokes

Whales have two powerful sets of muscles to help them move their tails up and down. The strongest set of muscles is used to move the tail up. This movement is known as the power stroke, as it pushes the whale through the water.

Smooth swimmers

Water is much harder to move through than air. When you swim, water drags against your body and slows you down. Whales have oily skin, which helps the water to flow smoothly over them. Their blubber also moves around under their skin as they swim, which stops the water from dragging too much on their bodies.

This diagram shows how a dolphin uses its tail to push itself through the water.

On the power stroke, the dolphin's tail moves up.

The force makes the dolphin's body move down and along.

The dolphin lowers its tail, and the front of its body rises up, ready to begin another power stroke.

Whale out of water

Whales often throw themselves into the air head-first and fall back into the water with a splash. This is known as breaching. No one is sure why they do this. It could be to signal to each other, to look for food above the water, or just to have fun.

Internet links

For links to exciting websites about this subject, go to **www.usborne-quicklinks.com** and enter the keywords "discovery whales".

This killer whale is breaching. Whales breach by swimming to the surface and using their powerful muscles to propel themselves out of the water.

Stiff necks

Most whales have short, stiff necks, so they can only move their heads up and down, not from side to side. This stops their heads from swaying around as they swim, which would slow them down. To look around, whales have to turn their entire bodies in the water, using their flippers and tail flukes.

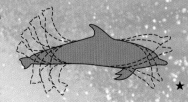

This side-view shows how far a dolphin can move its head and tail up and down.

 Fact: An Olympic swimmer may reach speeds of 9kph (6mph), but in short bursts some whales can go as fast as 56kph (35mph).

Basic senses

Whales have four basic senses, which are well suited to their underwater lives. They have sight, touch, taste and hearing as other mammals do, but, unlike other mammals, most whales have no sense of smell.

Hearing

When sound travels, it causes vibrations. Like all mammals, whales hear sounds by detecting these vibrations with ears inside their heads. Some vibrations reach their ears through small openings just behind each eye, but most sound travels to their ears by vibrating along their lower jaws.

These are bottlenose dolphins. Bottlenose dolphins often touch each other with their snouts and flippers to say hello.

Touch

Whales have sensitive skin, so they are very aware of touch. They use touch to communicate with each other. Dolphins often show other dolphins they are friends by rubbing bellies with them, or by patting each other with their flippers.

Taste

Whales' tongues are sensitive to taste. They may use their sense of taste to decide what food to eat. Scientists think whales may also be able to taste chemicals from other whales, to tell if they are friendly or not.

Above and below

Most whales have good eyesight, and some whales can adjust their eyes to see almost as well in air as in water. Whales often poke their heads above the surface of the water to have a look around. This is known as spyhopping.

Internet links

For links to exciting websites about whale senses, go to **www.usborne-quicklinks.com** and enter the keywords "discovery whales".

Sea sight

All animals need light in order to see, but most whales can see well even in dark, murky water. At the back of whales' eyes is a reflective layer, called a tapetum. This layer reflects light back into their eyes, helping them to make better use of any dim light in the water.

★

This is a cutaway diagram of a whale's eye from the side.

Light enters the eye here.

The blue layer is sensitive to light.

The red layer is the tapetum, which reflects light back onto the light-sensitive layer.

This humpback whale may be spyhopping to look for fish or other whales.

Fact: Whales' eyes produce a constant trickle of oily tears. The tears wash away dirt and help stop their eyes from becoming infected.

Underwater sounds

Sound is very important to whales. They have developed a way of using sound to find their way around and to hunt for food. Whales also use sound to keep in touch with each other.

Seeing with sound

As they swim, toothed whales make high-pitched clicking noises, which bounce off objects in their path. The time it takes for the clicks to bounce back tells a whale how far away an object is. Whales can also work out the object's shape and size from the direction of the returning clicks. This way of using sound is called echolocation.

Melon heads

Toothed whales produce clicks by forcing air back and forth through hollow tubes in their heads. Most toothed whales have a fatty lump, called a melon, in their foreheads. The clicks pass through the melon, which focuses them into a narrow beam, and aims them in the right direction.

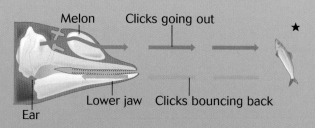

Melon   Clicks going out

Ear   Lower jaw   Clicks bouncing back

This diagram shows how a dolphin finds fish by sending out clicks. Vibrations caused by the clicks travel back along the dolphin's lower jaw to its ear.

Scientists think whales probably have to learn to use echolocation. This young dusky dolphin may learn how to use echolocation by copying its mother.

Fact: A dolphin using echolocation could pick out an object the size of a table tennis ball from almost the length of a soccer field away.

High and low sounds

Sound travels in invisible waves. High sounds create lots of closely packed waves and low sounds create spread-out waves. Toothed whales use high sounds for echolocation, as the shape of the waves means they hit small objects in their path. Baleen whales can't make high sounds, but may use low sounds to find large objects.

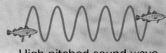
High-pitched sound wave

This shows how high sounds are good for detecting small fish.

Low-pitched sound wave

This shows how low sounds are likely to miss small fish.

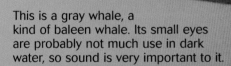
This is a gray whale, a kind of baleen whale. Its small eyes are probably not much use in dark water, so sound is very important to it.

Keeping in touch

Sound travels five times faster through water than it does through air, so it is a good way for whales to keep in touch over long distances. Some scientists think the low-pitched sounds made by baleen whales can travel up to 5,500km (3,500 miles).

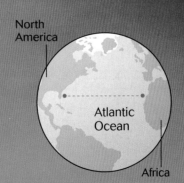
North America

Atlantic Ocean

Africa

The red dots on this map represent baleen whales. A baleen whale near the coast of North America could be heard by a baleen whale near the coast of Africa.

Dolphin brains

Many people think dolphins are very intelligent. From studying dolphins in captivity, we know more about their intelligence than that of any other whale family. But scientists still have a lot to learn about the intelligence of wild dolphins.

Brain size

Dolphins have larger brains for their body size than any other animals except people. Bottlenose dolphins have the largest brains for their size. However, dolphins may need large brains for echolocation, rather than for things we see as signs of intelligence, such as language.

Catching prey

In the wild, dolphins have developed clever ways of hunting for food. Bottlenose dolphins, for example, sometimes work together to drive fish onto the shore, where they are easier to catch.

Dolphins force the fish onto the shore, so the fish can't escape.

Then the dolphins quickly leap onto the beach to eat the fish.

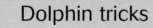

Dolphin tricks

Dolphins in captivity quickly learn to respond to instructions from their trainers, so they can perform tricks on command, such as leaping through hoops or doing somersaults.

This bottlenose dolphin is being trained to leap through a hoop as a part of a routine for a show.

Using sound

Dolphins can use sounds to pass information to each other. In one experiment with dolphins in captivity, a dolphin passed instructions to another dolphin in a separate pool, telling it which of two buttons to press to find food.

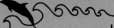

Internet links

For links to exciting websites about this subject, go to **www.usborne-quicklinks.com** and enter the keywords "discovery whales".

This shows how a dolphin would use its snout to press buttons.

Whales can learn to respond to both sounds and gestures. These pilot whales are learning to leap out of the water when their trainer raises his hand.

Dolphin whistles

Every dolphin can make a special whistling sound, known as a signature whistle, which it uses to identify itself. Dolphins can also copy each others' signature whistles. Some scientists think that dolphins may use other dolphins' signature whistles to call for them.

Fact: Dolphins can recognize their reflections in a mirror; the only other animals that can do this are chimpanzees and people.

Breathing

All animals need a gas called oxygen in order to live. Like people, whales get oxygen by taking in air, so they must come to the water's surface to breathe. But whales also have ways of being able to stay underwater for long periods of time.

You can clearly see the open blowholes on these spotted dolphins, as they come up to the surface to breathe.

Taking in air

At the surface, whales open their blowholes and take as much air as possible into their lungs. The more air they can take in and the more oxygen they absorb, the longer they can stay underwater. Before diving underwater, whales close their blowholes to stop any water from getting in.

Whale blows

When whales breathe out, a cloud of spray, or blow, appears above the water. The blow is mainly made up of the whale's breath, which becomes visible when it hits cold air, like your breath on a cold day. It also contains water that has been trapped around the blowhole.

★

Humpback whale

Blue whale

Right whale

Sperm whale

Minke whale

These pictures are head-on views, showing different whales' blows. By looking at the size and shape of the blow, it is possible to tell what kind of whale made it.

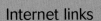

Internet links

For links to exciting websites about how whales and dolphins breath, go to **www.usborne-quicklinks.com** and enter the keywords "discovery whales".

 Fact: Blue whales have the tallest blow. It can be up to 12m (39ft) high, which is about the same height as a building with three floors.

Lasting longer

Although whales need to come to the surface to breathe, they can store extra oxygen in their blood and muscles. This enables them to stay underwater after using up the oxygen in their lungs. During dives, their hearts beat more slowly than when they are just swimming along, which helps them use up less oxygen.

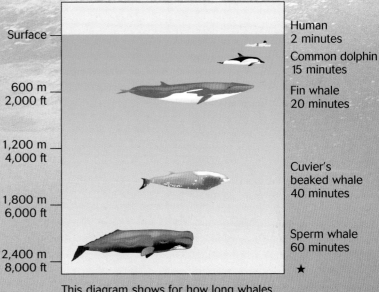

Surface

600 m
2,000 ft

1,200 m
4,000 ft

1,800 m
6,000 ft

2,400 m
8,000 ft

Human
2 minutes

Common dolphin
15 minutes

Fin whale
20 minutes

Cuvier's beaked whale
40 minutes

Sperm whale
60 minutes

★

This diagram shows for how long whales usually dive, and the different depths they can reach, compared to people.

Diving deeper

The deeper you go underwater, the more water presses down on you from above. This is called water pressure. If people dived deeper than 150m (490ft), their chests and lungs would be crushed by the pressure of the water. Whales can dive much deeper than this because they have flexible chests and lungs, which can cave in and then return to their normal shape.

These pilot whales are diving to catch squid. They can dive six times deeper than people.

17

Feeding

Toothed whales and baleen whales eat different foods and feed in very different ways. Most toothed whales hunt for animals such as fish and squid, and catch them with their teeth. Baleen whales eat smaller animals and use their baleen plates to trap their food.

Teeth and eating

Whales' teeth are shaped to help them catch their prey (the animals they hunt). Dolphins have sharp teeth which are good for gripping fish, while killer whales have large, strong teeth for biting chunks of meat off larger prey.

This is an Amazon river dolphin. They can have up to 140 teeth in their long snouts.

Internet links

For links to exciting websites about this subject, go to **www.usborne-quicklinks.com** and enter the keywords "discovery whales".

Fish balls

Dolphins often hunt together for fish. One way they do this is to swim beneath a group of fish, forcing the fish to the surface. Then they swim around the fish until all the fish are packed together in a ball. Finally, each dolphin swims through the fish ball, eating as many fish as it can.

Dolphins herd fish into a ball by swimming around them like this.

Baleen whale food

Baleen whales eat small fish, shrimp-like creatures called krill and tiny animals called zooplankton. Some zooplankton are so tiny they can only be seen through a magnifying glass. In order to survive, baleen whales have to eat huge amounts. A blue whale can eat up to 4,000kg (8,800lb) of food a day, which is about the same weight as 12,000 pizzas.

This humpback whale is feeding on fish near the surface. The birds around it are waiting to catch any fish that might leap out of the water.

Baleen plates

Massive mouthfuls

A baleen whale feeds by filling its mouth with water that is packed with fish and zooplankton. Then it closes its mouth and lifts its tongue, forcing the water out through the baleen plates. The baleen plates act like a sieve, letting out the water but trapping the food in the whale's mouth. The whale then picks out the food with its tongue and swallows it.

A baleen whale swims along with its mouth open, until its mouth is filled with sea water and food.

Then the whale closes its mouth, pushing the water out through its baleen plates before swallowing the food.

Fact: Dolphins, and most other toothed whales, swallow their food whole, without chewing it first.

Finding a mate

In order to produce babies, whales first have to find a mate (a whale of the opposite sex). Some whales have to travel thousands of miles for this, and some male whales have to fight for a mate.

These two gray whales are making their way to Mexico, where they go every year to find mates.

Loners

Baleen whales mostly live alone and are often far apart from other members of their species. They have special sites where they meet up at the same time each year to find mates.

Wandering males

Most toothed whales live in groups and find mates within their group. Sperm whales, however, have separate male and female groups. So males have to travel to search out female groups and find mates.

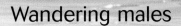

These are false killer whales. They live in groups with whales of both sexes, so finding mates is easy.

Love songs

Male humpback whales will sing alone for hours to attract a mate. Their songs are made up of groans, moans, trills and chirps. A singing male will swim back and forth in the same area, only stopping when it finds a female. They may also use their songs to try to warn off other males.

Kiss chase

Some whales have very active ways of attracting mates. Males and females will chase each other around in circles, touch one another with their flippers and bellies, and leap out of the water together.

These spotted dolphins are rubbing bellies to show they are interested in each other.

Fighting for females

Male whales sometimes fight each other over a female whale. Male narwhals, for example, each have a long single tusk which they use to battle with each other. The narwhal with the longest and strongest tusk usually wins.

These narwhals are crossing tusks as they fight over a female. They sometimes spear each other.

 Fact: Male humpback whales sing longer and more complicated songs than any other animal. The longest recorded humpback song lasted for 22 hours.

Whale babies

Baby whales grow inside their mothers. They are born underwater and look like small adults. Baby whales are known as calves.

Tail first

Calves are born with soft flukes and fins, making it easier for them to slip out at birth. They are usually born tail first, so the blowhole comes out last. This stops the calf from breathing in water.

The mother gives birth near the surface, so the calf does not have far to go to take its first breath.

Using her head and snout, the mother lifts the calf above the water like this, so it can breathe.

★

Mother's milk

★

This shows a calf feeding from its mother's teats, which are in a slit on her belly.

Mothers begin to feed their calves with milk a few hours after they are born. The milk contains lots of fat. The fat helps calves to develop a thick layer of blubber, which keeps them warm.

Internet links

For links to exciting websites about whale babies, go to **www.usborne-quicklinks.com** and enter the keywords "discovery whales".

This gray whale is teaching her calf how to spyhop. The calf looks like a small version of its mother.

Close contact

For the first few weeks of their lives, calves are weak, and stay close to their mothers for protection. Although calves can swim at birth, to begin with a calf may rest one of its flippers on its mother's body. This stops it from getting too tired.

A calf presses its flipper to its mother's side, so it can be helped along in the water.

This killer whale mother is with her two calves. Killer whale mothers and calves often stay together throughout the mothers' lives.

Protective mothers

Whale mothers are very protective of their calves. They guard them against predators (animals that eat other animals) such as sharks and killer whales. If a calf is wounded and unable to swim to the surface to breathe, the mother will hold it at the surface for as long as she can.

Staying together

Most calves stay with their mothers for two or three years, learning which predators to avoid and how to hunt for food. Calves also learn how to communicate with other whales, by copying the sounds their mothers make.

Fact: At birth, a whale is about a quarter of the length of its mother.

Living in groups

Most toothed whales live together in groups. There can be up to 500 whales in a group, depending on the species and where they live. Living in groups makes it easier for toothed whales to hunt for food and defend themselves. There are two main types of groups, known as schools and pods.

Schools and pods

The members of a school can vary from day to day, as whales move from one school to another. However, some species, such as killer whales, often live in fixed family groups and stay in those groups for their entire lives. These groups are known as pods.

Helping each other

Toothed whales in the open ocean form the largest schools, so they can spread out across the water and cover a greater area in their search for prey. When they find a group of fish, they often leap out of the water to let other members of their school know where it is.

Nursery groups

To protect their young, some toothed whale mothers live together in groups with their calves and adult females without calves, called aunts. These are known as nursery groups. Aunts take care of the calves while the mothers hunt for food.

This is a school of spotted dolphins. They usually live in small schools of between five and 15 dolphins.

Tail fights

Whales often try to help other members of their species if they are in danger. Sperm whales, for example, will surround a wounded whale or calf to try to stop it from being attacked. They drive off the attackers by beating their powerful tails up and down in the water.

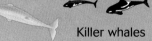

Sperm whales

Killer whales

This picture shows how sperm whales would surround sperm whale calves, to stop them from being attacked by a pod of killer whales.

 Fact: Male dolphins often form strong friendships. Pairs of male bottlenose dolphins have been known to stay together for up to 15 years.

Whale travel

Whales often travel long
distances to find food,
to mate or to give birth.
This is called migrating.

Finding their way

Deep inside the Earth there are very
hot metals, which are magnetic. These
metals create a magnetic pull, or force,
around the Earth. Scientists think whales
may be able to detect this force, and
use it to find their way on long
migrations across the oceans.

This is a humpback whale
mother and calf. After
giving birth in warmer waters,
humpback mothers return to
colder waters with their calves.

Long trips

Most baleen whales make long
migrations every year, from the warm
waters where they mate and give birth,
to colder waters where they feed.

Gray whales make one of the
longest migrations, from Mexico to
the Arctic — a round trip of around
20,000km (12,500 miles).

The arrows on this map show
where different groups
of humpback whales
travel each year.

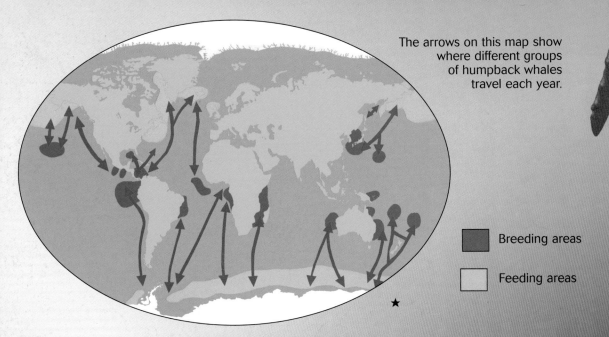

Breeding areas

Feeding areas

 26

Escaping the ice

Beluga whales are one of the few species of toothed whales that do migrate. Most beluga whales spend the summer in Arctic seas in the far north. In winter, these seas completely freeze over and the belugas are forced to travel south to less icy seas.

Staying at home

Very few species of toothed whales migrate, although they often move around over a wide area. The area in which a toothed whale regularly lives is known as its home range. A few toothed whales stay in the same small area all their lives.

These beluga whales are migrating south. Belugas travel in groups for protection against predators.

Fact: Over a lifetime of 40 years or more, a gray whale travels the same distance as from Earth to the Moon and back.

Whales and people

People have always been fascinated by whales. Since ancient times there have been stories about gentle and friendly dolphins helping people. Large whales, however, were often seen as terrifying, man-eating monsters.

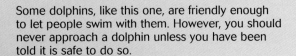

These dolphin paintings are on a wall in a palace in Knossos, Crete. They are about 3,500 years old.

Friendly dolphins

Dolphins are very curious and, unlike many other wild animals, sometimes go out of their way to approach people. Some dolphins even live apart from other dolphins and close to people, often staying in the same area for many years. They may have become separated from their group, or they could just enjoy being with people.

Some dolphins, like this one, are friendly enough to let people swim with them. However, you should never approach a dolphin unless you have been told it is safe to do so.

Dolphin myth

There is an ancient Greek myth about a dolphin saving a musician named Arion, who was thrown into the sea by pirates. Arion charmed the dolphin with his music, and was carried to shore on its back.

Dolphins to the rescue

There are lots of true stories of dolphins protecting people from sharks. For example, in 1992 a woman was swimming off the coast of Tonga, in the Pacific, when a large shark appeared. Within moments, the woman was surrounded by dolphins, which stayed with her until the shark swam away.

Hunted whales

In the past, whales were hunted for their blubber, meat and oil. However, people's attitudes to whales are changing. Hunting whales is now banned in most countries, and whale watching has become very popular. There are rules about how to approach whales, so the whales are not disturbed.

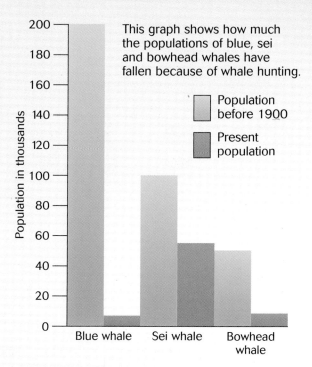

This gray whale is being patted by whale watchers. Gray whales are especially curious whales and often approach boats.

This graph shows how much the populations of blue, sei and bowhead whales have fallen because of whale hunting.

Population in thousands

| Population before 1900 |
| Present population |

Blue whale   Sei whale   Bowhead whale

Internet links

For links to exciting websites about this subject, go to **www.usborne-quicklinks.com** and enter the keywords "discovery whales".

Threats today

Whales still face many threats from people. Poisonous waste dumped into the sea can build up inside whales' bodies and damage their health. The biggest threat to dolphins is from fishing nets. Thousands of dolphins die each year when they get tangled up in fishing nets and drown.

 Fact: The ancient Greeks believed it was almost as bad to kill a dolphin as it was to kill another person.

Enormous whales

Some of the largest baleen whales belong to a family called rorqual whales. Blue whales are a kind of rorqual whale, and are the longest, loudest and heaviest animals ever to have lived.

Groovy throats

All rorqual whales have folds of skin, known as throat grooves, that run from underneath the lower jaw to behind their flippers. These throat grooves can unfold to make their mouths bigger, so the rorqual whales can take in huge mouthfuls of fish, zooplankton and water while they are feeding.

The whale takes in gulps of sea water and food. The weight forces the grooves to unfold.

The whale closes its mouth and tightens its grooves, forcing water out through its baleen plates.

This blue whale is feeding. You can see the water being forced out of its mouth.

Water support

Rorqual whales are able to grow so enormous, and so much larger than land animals, because they live in water. Water helps to support the weight of their bodies. Large whales couldn't survive for long on land, as the weight of their bodies would crush their lungs, so they wouldn't be able to breathe.

This is a blue whale's tail. Blue whales' tail flukes are about 8m (26ft) wide — the width of 3 buses parked side by side.

Unusual whales

Humpback whales are a little different from the rest of the rorqual whale family. The other rorqual whales have long, slender bodies, but humpback whales have shorter, fatter bodies, and much longer flippers. They also have an unusual way of catching fish, using bubbles to trap them. This is known as bubble-netting.

The whale circles beneath a group of fish, blowing bubbles. These form a kind of net, which traps the fish in the middle.

The whale then swims up through the bubble-net with its mouth open, and gulps down the fish.

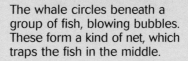
Fact: A single breath from a blue whale could blow up 2,000 balloons.

Right and gray whales

Right whales and gray whales are large baleen whales, and are closely related to each other. There are three kinds of right whales, but only one kind of gray whale.

Sailing in the wind

Right whales and gray whales are some of the most active whales, and often breach and spyhop. Southern right whales sometimes raise their tail flukes above the water and use them as sails, allowing themselves to be blown along by the wind. Scientists think they do this for fun, as they often swim back to the starting point and do it again.

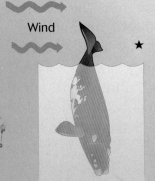

Wind

Right whales hold their tails at a right angle to the wind, in order to be blown along by it.

Right to hunt

Right whales were named by early whale hunters, who thought they were the "right" whales to hunt. They are slow swimmers and float to the surface after being killed, which made them easier to catch and handle.

Surface feeders

Right whales don't have throat grooves like rorqual whales, so they can't take in huge gulps of water. Instead, they feed by swimming at, or near, the surface of the water, with their mouths open. Once enough food has collected on the inside of their baleen plates, they pick it off with their tongues and swallow it.

This is a southern right whale. They only live in oceans in the southern half of the world.

Whale lice

Whales have tiny animals called lice living and feeding on their skin. Being slow swimmers, right whales and gray whales have more lice than other whales, as lice can stay attached to their skin more easily. Some right whales also have hard growths of skin on their heads, known as callosites, which lice live on.

This gray whale may be breaching to try to knock lice off its skin.

These callosites are white because the lice that live on them are white. Lice can also be pink and orange and turn the callosites different shades.

Messy eaters

Gray whales have an unusual way of feeding. They roll onto their sides and suck up mud and water containing small, shrimp-like creatures from the sea floor. The gray whales then push out the mud and water through their baleen plates.

When feeding, gray whales stir up the sea floor, like this.

Internet links

For links to exciting websites about this subject, go to **www.usborne-quicklinks.com** and enter the keywords "discovery whales".

Fact: Bowhead whales, a kind of right whale, live longer than other whales. The oldest recorded bowhead whale lived to be 130 years old.

Deep-water whales

Sperm whales and beaked whales can dive for longer and go deeper than other whales. Scientists think sperm whales may be able to dive as deep as 3,000m (9,800ft).

Tail power

This is a bottlenose whale, a kind of beaked whale. Bottlenose whales can dive for about an hour.

Bottlenose whales can dive for as long as sperm whales, but sperm whales can dive much deeper. This is partly because sperm whales have especially large tail flukes for their size. Sperm whales use their flukes to power themselves through the water at speeds of up to 3m (10ft) a second.

Waxy heads

Sperm whales have an oily wax, known as spermaceti oil, in their heads. Some scientists think sperm whales can cool the wax as they dive, making it solid and more closely packed together. This would help them to sink more quickly.

Sperm whales may also use the wax for echolocation. The wax could help to focus their clicks, and may even make the clicks loud enough to stun their prey.

This cutaway diagram shows the spermaceti oil in a sperm whale's head.

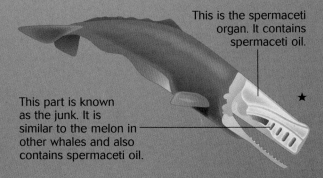

This is the spermaceti organ. It contains spermaceti oil.

This part is known as the junk. It is similar to the melon in other whales and also contains spermaceti oil.

Fact: A sperm whale's head is bigger than a car.

This Cuvier's beaked whale is covered in scars. Scientists think male beaked whales may fight each other a lot.

Mysterious whales

Beaked whales spend most of their lives in deep water far from land, and only briefly come up to the surface to breathe. This makes them very hard to study, so very little is known about them. Some species have only been seen when the animals die and are washed ashore.

This is a sperm whale. You can clearly see its large tail flukes.

Internet links

For links to exciting websites about deep water whales, go to **www.usborne-quicklinks.com** and enter the keywords "discovery whales".

Smaller sperm whales

The sperm whale has two much smaller relatives, the pygmy and dwarf sperm whales. When startled, these sperm whales sometimes squirt a cloudy red liquid into the water. They may do this to confuse their predators, while they quickly swim away.

This is a pygmy sperm whale. They grow to be about 3m (10ft) long.

Arctic whales

Narwhals and belugas are toothed whales and belong to the same family. Most narwhals and belugas live in the freezing waters of the Arctic.

Under the ice

Arctic waters are covered with ice for most of the year, so narwhals and belugas spend much of their time swimming under ice sheets. They have thick layers of blubber to keep them warm. To breathe, they have to swim up to holes in the ice. Belugas and narwhals can swim close below the ice because they don't have dorsal fins.

Burping belugas

This beluga whale has a rounded melon. Beluga whales' melons change shape as they make different sounds.

Belugas make a wider variety of noises than any other whale. They communicate with each other by making whistles, squawks, grunts and burps. Grunts, for example, may be used as warning sounds. Belugas have very large melons, which they might use to help them make different sounds.

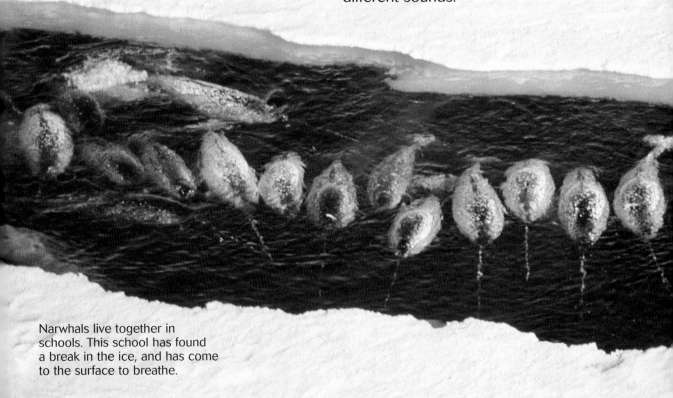

Narwhals live together in schools. This school has found a break in the ice, and has come to the surface to breathe.

Fact: Beluga whales make breathing holes by pushing against the ice with their heads. They can break through ice up to 10cm (4in) thick.

This beluga has pushed its melon to the front of its face. This may mean it is feeling aggressive.

Changing faces

When belugas change the shape of their melons and mouths, the expressions on their faces also change, and they can look as if they are smiling or frowning. Belugas may use their expressions to communicate with each other, but scientists aren't yet sure what the different expressions mean.

Internet links

For links to exciting websites about arctic whales, go to **www.usborne-quicklinks.com** and enter the keywords "discovery whales".

Tooth to tusk

Narwhals have very strange teeth. All narwhals are born with two teeth, but in male narwhals the left tooth keeps growing, until it forms a tusk up to 3m (10ft) long. Female narwhals occasionally grow a short tusk.

Male narwhals use their tusks to fight for females (see page 21). The male with the widest, strongest tusk is often the most important in his school.

★

This is what a narwhal's skull looks like. The tusk grows out from the upper jaw.

Oceanic dolphins

Oceanic dolphins can be found in seas and oceans all over the world, except for the coldest polar waters. There are 26 different species, including common, spinner and bottlenose dolphins.

Different dolphins

Some oceanic dolphins are much more curious and playful than others. Dusky dolphins, for example, often leap amazingly high out of the water and will approach boats and people. Rough-toothed dolphins are very shy and only stay briefly at the surface.

These are rough-toothed dolphins. They have narrower heads and larger flippers than other oceanic dolphins.

Leaping and breathing

Most dolphins that live far out at sea are fast swimmers. To avoid slowing down too much when they breathe, some dolphins take long, low leaps out of the water every time they want to take a breath. This is known as porpoising (although, in fact, porpoises rarely do it). It is faster than swimming along at the surface, as the water doesn't drag on their bodies and slow them down.

The dolphin swims up to the surface at high speed, ready to porpoise.

As it begins to leave the water, it opens its blowhole and takes a breath.

For a few seconds the dolphin's entire body comes out of the water.

★

The dolphin closes its blowhole, and re-enters the water head-first.

Fact: Spotted dolphins are born without spots. As they get older they develop more and more spots, and the spots get bigger.

Dolphin markings

Although some of the most common oceanic dolphins don't have clear markings on their bodies, most species have striking ones. About half of all oceanic dolphins have black and white markings and Atlantic white-sided dolphins also have yellow streaks on their tails. Some striped and bottlenose dolphins have bright pink patches on their bellies.

You can see the black and white markings on these dusky dolphins.

These bottlenose dolphins are looking for food on a coral reef. They can easily be studied here, as they are in clear water near land.

Bottlenose dolphins

Because many bottlenose dolphins live along coasts, more is known about them than about other oceanic dolphins. For example, we know that in bottlenose dolphin schools, mothers and calves spend most of their time together and that young males form groups of their own.

Killers and pilots

Killer whales and pilot whales belong to the dolphin family. Killer whales, or orcas, are the largest and fastest members of the dolphin family.

Killer whales are easily recognized by their clear black and white markings.

Naming killers

Killer whales are called killers because they eat other whales and dolphins, and will even attack blue whales, which are three times their size. But killer whales in the wild have never been known to attack humans. Killer whales have the most varied diet of any whale – they also eat fish, birds, turtles and seals.

Hunting on land

Killer whales are one of the few species of whales that pursue their prey onto land. Sea lions often sit closely packed together on beaches, so killer whales find it easiest to hunt them by throwing themselves onto the shore, and catching them in their jaws. Then they return to the water to eat their catch.

This killer whale is about to slide onto the shore in order to grab a sea lion. Killer whales have to be careful not to go too far or they will get stuck on land.

Girl power

Killer whales and some pilot whales live in pods of up to 40 whales. Most pod members are related to each other, and usually stay together for life. In many killer whale pods, the older females are in charge.

These are pygmy killer whales. They are closely related to killer whales and pilot whales, and also live in pods.

Internet links

For links to exciting websites about killer and pilot whales, go to **www.usborne-quicklinks.com** and enter the keywords "discovery whales".

Bad piloting

Every year, thousands of whales swim onto beaches and become stuck, or stranded. Pilot whales strand more than other whales, and often strand in large groups. This is probably because of the strong bonds between pod members.

When one member of the pod is ill, or has lost its sense of direction, it may strand. The others may not want to leave it, and so they become stranded themselves. Experts are needed to rescue stranded whales.

When the tide goes out, whales are sometimes left stranded on the beach like this.

Experts cover the whale with wet cloths, to keep it damp until it is returned to the water.

The whale is lifted onto a stretcher and carried back to the water.

 Fact: Killer whales have the tallest dorsal fins of any whale or dolphin. They can grow to be taller than a man.

River dolphins

River dolphins are only distantly related to oceanic dolphins. They have longer snouts and smaller eyes than other whales. River dolphins live in some of the largest and muddiest rivers in Asia and South America.

Living in rivers

River dolphins are slow swimmers and can't dive for more than a minute. This doesn't matter, as they feed on fish, prawns and crabs that live in the mud at the sides of rivers, close to the surface of the water. River dolphins have flat teeth at the back of their snouts, which they use to crush the hard shells of crabs and prawns.

Blind and hairy ★

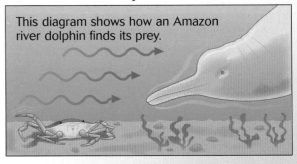

This diagram shows how an Amazon river dolphin finds its prey.

As a crab moves in the water, it creates small waves. These waves are felt by hairs on the dolphin's snout, helping the dolphin to find the crab.

Most river dolphins have poor eyesight, and some are blind. However, good eyesight would be useless to them in the muddy waters where they live. River dolphins use other senses to find their way around and hunt for food. Amazon river dolphins have short hairs on their snouts, which are sensitive to movements in the water. All river dolphins have a well-developed sense of echolocation.

This is an Amazon river dolphin. It has very large flippers, which it can trail along the river bed to feel for animals to eat.

Swimming among trees

During the rainy months of the year, the forests along the Amazon river, in South America, and the Yangtze river, in China, become flooded. When this happens, the river dolphins move to the flooded areas to find food. They can swim between the trees as they have flexible necks and flippers.

Internet links

For links to exciting websites about river dolphins, go to **www.usborne-quicklinks.com** and enter the keywords "discovery whales".

This is a Yangtze river dolphin. It is the only kind of river dolphin which has a snout that turns up at the end.

Dolphins in danger

River dolphins are in danger of dying out. People are draining the rivers where the dolphins live and are catching so many fish that there are not enough left for the dolphins to eat. The most endangered dolphins are Yangtze river dolphins. There are fewer than 200 left.

This box shows the part of the Yangtze river where Yangtze river dolphins live.

China

Yangtze River

La Plata dolphins

La Plata dolphins are very unusual river dolphins. They share the same features as other river dolphins, but never go into rivers. They live in shallow waters off the coast of South America. La Plata dolphins grow to be about 2m (7ft) long.

Fact: Fishermen call La Plata dolphins "white ghosts" because they have pale bodies and dart away when they see humans.

Amazing facts

Whales are amazing animals. Here you can find out some fascinating facts about them.

This is a pink Indo-Pacific humpback dolphin.

Indo-Pacific humpback dolphins are among the strangest-looking dolphins. Their skin can be white, or even pink.

A blue whale's heart is the same size as a small car.

Spinner dolphins can spin around as many as seven times in the air without stopping.

A spinner dolphin twists around in the air as it leaps out of the water.

Until the 17th century, many people believed that narwhal tusks were unicorn horns. They were sold in Europe for lots of money and were thought to have magical and healing powers.

Scientists can recognize individual whales by looking at scars on their dorsal fins and tail flukes. Humpback whales can be recognized from the individual patterns on their tail flukes.

Whales never go completely to sleep. They sleep by "switching off" half of the brain at a time. They need to keep the other half of the brain switched on in order to breathe.

Right whale mothers often swim on their backs with their newborn calves resting on their bellies. The mothers cuddle their calves with their flippers.

The white stripe on this minke whale's flipper tells us it probably lives in northern oceans.

Minke whales that live in northern oceans have white stripes on their flippers. But most of the minke whales in southern oceans have no stripes on their flippers.

Whales often surf the waves in front of ships to help them swim faster. This is known as bow-riding (a bow is the front of a ship).

Most rorqual whales only feed during the summer. They can store fat from their food in their blubber and muscle, and live off this fat for the rest of the year.

Near the coast of Laguna, in Brazil, local bottlenose dolphins help the fishermen catch fish. The dolphins drive the fish in the direction of the beach, where the fishermen wait with their nets. Any fish that turn around to escape the nets swim straight into the mouths of the dolphins.

An elephant could fit on a blue whale's tongue.

You can tell the age of some whales by looking at the layers in their teeth. There is roughly one layer for each year of their lives.

Whale calves are born with a light covering of hair on their bodies, but they lose this after a few weeks.

Sperm whales produce a dark, foul-smelling, waxy substance called ambergris in their guts. When heated, ambergris smells sweet, and until the 1980s it was used in many countries to make perfume.

Dall's porpoises often swim extremely fast just below the surface of the water. As they swim, they create fan-shaped splashes known as rooster tails.

Scientists call whales, dolphins and porpoises "cetaceans", which comes from the Greek word *ketos*, meaning sea monster.

This is a Dall's porpoise. Although smaller than most other whales, Dall's porpoises are very fast swimmers.

Index

Words with several pages sometimes have a number in **bold** to show where to find the main explanation. Page numbers in *italic* show where to find pictures.

Amazon river dolphins, *18, 42*
ambergris, 45
Atlantic white-sided dolphins, 39
aunts, 25
baby whales *see* calves
baleen plates, *6,* 18, 19, 32, 33
baleen whales, 4, 6, 7, 13, 18, 19, 20, 26, 30, 32
beaked whales, 4, 34, 35
beluga whales, 4, 5, *27,* **36–37**
birth, 22
blowholes, **7**, 16, 22, 38
blows, 16
blubber, **6**, 8, 22, 29, 36
blue whales, 5, 19, 29, *30, 31,* 40, 44, 45
bottlenose dolphins, *2, 4, 6, 10, 14, 39,* 45
bottlenose whales, *34*
bowhead whales, 29, 33
bow-riding, 45
brains, 5, 14
breaching, 9, 32, 33
breathing, 4, **16–17**, 36
bubble-netting, *31*
callosites, *33*
calves, **22–23**, 25, 44
    hair on bodies, 45
captivity, 14, 15
cetaceans, 45
common dolphins, *17,* 38
communication, 10, 13, 23, 36, 37
Cuvier's beaked whales, *17, 35*
Dall's porpoises, *45*
diving, *17,* 34
dorsal fins, 7, 44
dusky dolphins, *12,* 38, *39*
dwarf sperm whales, 35
ears, 6, 10
echolocation, 12, 13, 34
endangered dolphins, 43
eyes, *11*
false killer whales, *20*
feeding, **18–19**, 22, *30, 31,* 32, 33, 45

fighting, 21, 25
fin whales, *17*
fish, 4, 7, 13, 14, 18, 31, 40, 42, 43, 45
fish balls, 18
fishing nets, 29, 45
flippers, **7**, 8, 9, 23, 42, 43
gray whales, 4, 6, *13, 20–21, 22, 26,* 32, *33*
groups, 20, 24–25
hearts, 17
home range, 27
humpback whales, *1, 6, 11, 19,* 20, *26–27,* 31, 44
hunting
    people hunting whales, 29, 32
    whales hunting for food, 12, 13, 14, 18, 24, 40, 42
Indo-Pacific humpback dolphins, *44*
intelligence, 5, **14–15**
jaws, 10, 12, *37*
killer whales, *9,* 18, *23,* 24, *25,* **40–41**
krill, 19
La Plata dolphins, 43
lice, 33
lungs, 16, 17
magnetic force, 26
mammals, 4
markings, 39
mates, 20–21
melons, *12,* 36, 37
migrating, 26–27
milk, 22
minke whales, *45*
mouths, 6, 7, 19, 30, 32, 37
muscles, 8, 17
myths, 28
narwhals, 4, *21, 36–37,* 44
    tusks, 21, 37
necks, 9, 43
nursery groups, 25
oceanic dolphins, 38–39
orcas *see* killer whales
pilot whales, *15, 17,* 40, 41
pods, **24**, 41
porpoises, 4, 5, 38
porpoising, 38
power strokes, 8
predators, 23

prey, **18**, 24, 40, 42
pygmy killer whales, *41*
pygmy right whales, 4
pygmy sperm whales, *35*
right whales, 4, **32–33**, 44
river dolphins, 4, *18,* **42–43**
rooster tails, 45
rorqual whales, 4, **30–31**, 45
rough-toothed dolphins, *38*
sailing, 32
schools, **24**, 37, 39
sei whales, 29
senses
    hearing, 10
    sight, **11**, 42
    taste, 10
    touch, **10**, 21
sharks, 4, 7, 28
signature whistles, 15
skin, 5, 6, 8, 10, 33
sleep, 44
snouts, 6, 42
sounds, **12–13**, 15, 23, 36
    clicks, 12, 34
    songs, 20
    whistles, 15, 36
sperm whales, *4–5, 17,* 25, **34–35**, 45
spermaceti oil, 34
spinner dolphins, 38, *44*
spotted dolphins, *8, 21, 25*
spyhopping, **11**, 22, 32
stranding, 41
striped dolphins, 39
swimming, **8–9**
    oceanic dolphins, 38
    people swimming with dolphins, 28
    river dolphins, 43
tails, *1, 7,* 8, 25
    tail flukes, 7, 9, 32, 34, 44
tapetum, 11
teeth, 4, 6, 18, 37, 42, 45
threats to whales, 29
throat grooves, 30
tongues, 10, 19, 45
toothed whales, 4, 6, 7, 12, 13, 18, 20, 24, 25, 27, 36
whale watching, 29
Yangtze river dolphins, *43*
zooplankton, 19, 30

Usborne Quicklinks

The Usborne Quicklinks Website is packed with links
to all the best websites on the Internet.

www.usborne-quicklinks.com

You'll find links to websites with:

- Homework help
- Information for projects and coursework
- Video and sound clips
- Quizzes and exercises
- Animated lessons and explanations
- Educational games
- Downloadable pictures
- Pronunciation guides

The websites and links are regularly reviewed and updated.

For homework, research or just for fun, the Usborne Quicklinks
Website saves time and take you straight to relevant,
reliable and exciting websites.

Internet links for this book
For the links and downloadable pictures for this book, go to

www.usborne-quicklinks.com

and enter the keywords **discovery whales**

When using the internet, make sure you follow the internet safety
guidelines displayed on the Usborne Quicklinks Website.

******

Acknowledgements

Every effort has been made to trace the copyright holders of the material in this book. If any rights have been omitted, the publishers offer to rectify this in any subsequent editions following notification. The publishers are grateful to the following organizations and individuals for their permission to reproduce material (t=top, m=middle, b=bottom, l=left, r=right):

Cover © Tom Brakefield/Corbis; © Digital Vision; **p1** François Gohier/Ardea; **p2** © Flip Nicklin/Minden Pictures/FLPA; **p4–5** (t) © Jorg & Petra Wegner/Bruce Coleman The Natural World, (b) François Gohier/Ardea; **p6** (bl) Ben Cropp/Ardea, (br) François Gohier/Ardea; **p6–7** (t) © Amos Nachoum/The Image Bank; **p8** © Digital Vision; **p9** © FLPA/Gerard Laoz; **p10** © Flip Nicklin/Minden Pictures/FLPA; **p11** © Johnny Johnson/Bruce Coleman The Natural World; **p12** © NHPA/A.N.T.; **p13** © Flip Nicklin/Minden Pictures/FLPA; **p14** © Powerstock; **p15** © Dave G. Houser/CORBIS; **p16** (t) © Pacific Stock/Bruce Coleman The Natural World; **p17** © NHPA/A.N.T.; **p18** © Flip Nicklin/Minden Pictures/FLPA; **p19** © Flip Nicklin/Minden Pictures/FLPA; **p20** (b) Kurt Amsler/Ardea; **p20–21** © NHPA/Norbert Wu; **p21** (m) Denize Herzing/Ardea, (b) © Flip Nicklin/Minden Pictures/FLPA; **p22** François Gohier/Ardea; **p23** © NHPA/Gerard Lacz; **p24–25** © Pacific Stock/Bruce Coleman The Natural World; **p26–27** © Pacific Stock/Bruce Coleman The Natural World; **p27** (b) © Sea World, Inc./CORBIS; **p28** (b) © Morton Beebe, S.F./CORBIS, (tr) © Kevin Schafer/CORBIS; **p29** © Pieter Folkens/Telegraph Colour Library; **p30** © Nature Picture Library/Doc White; **p31** © NHPA/David E. Myers; **p32–33** © Kim Westerkov/Stone; **p33** (tr) © Konrad Wothe/Minden Pictures/FLPA; **p34** (ml) © Sebastian Brennan/Marine Mammal Images; **p34–35** François Gohier/Ardea; **p35** (tr) © Nature Picture Library/Todd Pusser, (br) © Brian Chmielecki/Marine Mammal Images; **p36** (b) © Flip Nicklin/Minden Pictures/FLPA, (tr) © FLPA/F. W. Lane; **p37** (t) © Art Wolfe/Stone; **p38** © Jim Watt/Bruce Coleman The Natural World; **p39** (t) © Kim Westerkov/Stone, (b) © FLPA/Gerard Laoz; **p40** (t) © Brandon D. Cole/CORBIS, (b) D. Parer & E. Parer-Cook/Ardea; **p41** © Pacific Stock/Bruce Coleman The Natural World; **p42** © Flip Nicklin/Minden Pictures/FLPA; **p43** Nick Gordon/Ardea; **p44** (tl) © Hong Kong Dolphin Watch/Marine Mammal Images, (b) © Pacific Stock/Bruce Coleman The Natural World; **p45** (t) François Gohier/Ardea, (b) © S. Sinclair/Earthviews/FLPA; all fact boxes © Digital Vision

Series editor: Gillian Doherty; Editor: Rosie Dickins; Managing designer: Mary Cartwright
Digital image processing by John Russell and Emma Julings; Cover Design: Helen Edmonds
Additional design: Neil Francis; Additional consultant: Dr. Frances Dipper